Double Take

LANGUAGE PRACTICE

Listening and Speaking

Joanne Collie

2

Oxford University Press

Oxford University Press
Great Clarendon Street, Oxford OX2 6DP

Oxford New York

Athens Auckland Bangkok Bogota Bombay
Buenos Aires Calcutta Cape Town Dar es Salaam
Delhi Florence Hong Kong Istanbul Karachi
Kuala Lumpur Madras Madrid Melbourne
Mexico City Nairobi Paris Singapore
Taipei Tokyo Toronto Warsaw

and associated companies in
Berlin Ibadan

OXFORD and OXFORD ENGLISH
are trade marks of Oxford University Press

ISBN 0 19 432005 7

© Oxford University Press 1996

First published 1996
Fifth impression 1997

No unauthorized photocopying

Typeset by DP Press Ltd, Sevenoaks, Kent

Printed in Hong Kong

Acknowledgements

The author and publishers would like to thank the
following for their kind permission to reproduce
copyright material: Page 21 *Fish Tales* cartoon ©
Knight Features. Page 52 film stills: *Little Women*, Di
Novi/Columbia (Courtesy Kobal); *River Wild*,
Turman-Foster (Courtesy Kobal); *Frankenstein*, Tri-
Star/American Zoetrope (Courtesy Kobal). Page 54
War of the Buttons Enigma/David Appleby (Courtesy
Warner Brothers).

Illustrations by: Kathy Baxter, Rachel Busch, Stefan
Chabluk, Joan Corlass, Leo Duff, Nicki Elson, Neil
Gower, Robina Green, Michael Hill, Janek Matysiak,
Charmaine Peters, George Platt, Philip Reeve, Tim
Slade, Martin Ursall, Sholto Walker, with additional
material by DP Press.

Studio photography by: Mark Mason.
Location photography by: Gareth Boden, John
Walmsley.

The publishers would like to thank the following for
permission to reproduce photographs: Airwair,
Barnabys, Bauer, Bord Failte, Bradmet Catering by
permission of Bradford Education, Bubbles, Carrati
Sport Ltd, John Cleare, Collections, Collections/John
and Eliza Forder, C M Dixon, Finest Brands Int,
Flipside Projects/Clover Clothing, Formula One,
Image Bank, Innovations, MOMI, Outdoor Leisure,
Planet Earth, Tony Stone, SMPC, SMP/All Sport/M
Prior, Sowester Ltd, John Walmsley, Zefa.

The author would like to thank Cathy Hall and
Diane Hall for their support throughout the
development of these materials.

Contents

Symbols

 = Listen to the cassette

 = Speaking practice

Map of the book

Unit	Topic	Listening skills	
1	Family relations: different generations	• Listening puzzle, noting key words • Listening for information/specific items • Listening for gist • Listening to match speakers and photos • Identifying speakers	
2	Cities	• Listening for gist: an interview • Predicting vocabulary • Listening for specific items • Listening and following a route • Listening and deducing the rules of a game • Listening and sequencing items • Listening to a song	
3	Stories: a radio drama	• Listening for gist: an announcement • Listening for specific items • Identifying speakers, actions, phrases to request repetition • Discriminating between true/false statements • Interpreting intonation (anger) • Guessing meaning from context • Checking predictions	
4	Sports and hobbies	• Intensive listening: to solve a puzzle • Identifying mood of speakers/understanding enthusiasm, dislike, certainty, uncertainty • Listening for specific phrases • Listening and completing notes • Identifying percentages	
5	Wonstonia Mission: a space story	• Listening for gist and identifying a specific emotion • Understanding opinions • Listening for specific qualities • Listening for gist • Discriminating between certainty/uncertainty	
6	Strange but true stories	• Listening for gist and matching with pictures • Deducing the rules of a game • Listening for confirmation • Listening and sequencing • Listening for prediction and confirmation • Listening for detail	
7	Appearances and fashion accessories	• Predicting vocabulary • Understanding an advertisement • Listening for information • Understanding and carrying out instructions	

Speaking skills	Vocabulary	Language base
• Describing appearance • Describing experiences/events • Discussing/negotiating choices • Role-play: a radio interview	Family members Adjectives for describing people	Revision of Level 1 Language base
• Describing a route • Giving a guided tour • Chain game: creating complete sentences • Information exchange: requesting and giving information	Facilities in towns Activities in towns Giving directions WORD EQUIVALENCES	Revision of present simple time *can/can't*
• Retelling a story • Predicting and discussing • Preparing and giving a short summary/introduction • Discussing possible courses of action • Creating and narrating a sequence of events	Radio drama: characters, plot, implied setting Hairdressing Phrases to request repetition	Revision of simple past *could/couldn't* (possessive pronouns)
• Expressing certainty, uncertainty, enthusiasm, dislike • Information exchange: description/asking for repetition or clarification • Requesting and displaying information • Expressing plans and intentions	Kite flying Sports activities, exercises for fitness Plans and intentions	Present simple and present continuous Present continuous with future meaning
• Predicting and discussing • Negotiating/reporting decisions • Role-play: preparing, presenting and discussing a short improvised dialogue	Space and space travel Phrases to request a person's views, agreeing/disagreeing Leadership qualities	Modal verbs *will/won't, must/mustn't, need to/needn't*
• Making up and telling a short story • Narrating events in the past/negotiating choices • Panel game: telling stories • Information exchange: solving a mystery	Unusual stories IDIOMATIC LANGUAGE	Past continuous with *when/while* Past continuous contrasted with past simple
• Comparing and contrasting personal features, and summarizing them • Reporting and discussing choices • Preparing and giving a short product advertisement • Discussing/negotiating	Watches and other jewellery Footwear COLLOCATIONS	Regular + irregular comparative and superlative adjs. *too + adj* *a pair of*

Unit	Topic	Listening skills	
8	Holidays and travel	• Understanding questions and relating them to pictures • Listening for gist • Listening for specific items • Identifying problems and solutions/ understanding apologies • Listening to a song	
9	Food	• Listening for specific items • Using context to understand meaning • Predicting, listening for confirmation • Understanding and answering questions • Undertstanding and sequencing events in a factual narrative • Listening puzzle	
10	Disaster and survival	• Listening for specific items • Using context to understand meaning • Discriminating between obligation/no obligation • Listening for gist • Listening for information • Listening and making notes	
11	Treasure hunting	• Listening for gist • Listening for passive contructions • Listening for key words/specific information • Listening and following a route • Identifying emotions	
12	Film-making	• Understanding factual information, noting key words • Using context to understand meaning • Listening for key/technical words • Listening for gist • Listening and ordering	

Speaking skills	Vocabulary	Language base
• Exchanging personal information • Narrating and reacting • Guessing game: whose holiday? • Making apologies • Information exchange: booking holidays and apologising	Types of holiday Phrases to react to stories Phrases to apologise COLLOCATIONS	Present perfect with *ever/never*, *not yet/already*
• Comparing experiences and opinions • Asking questions and discussing answers • Agreeing a sequence • Exchanging views • Preparing a short report about a discussion	Sweets and sugar consumption School meals	Present perfect with *for* and *since* Present perfect contrasted with present simple
• Role-play: an interview • Retelling a story • Information exchange: completing gaps and making a joint decision • Describing a scene of action • Discussion/role-play • Exchanging ideas	Protective sports equipment Expressing worry/ reassurance Emergencies and survival	Countable and uncountable nouns with *some/any* Other determiners: *much/ many, a few/ a little*
• Predicting • Role-play: a news report • Negotiating decisions • Giving and responding to directions	Treasure hunting at sea/on land	Passive forms: present past and future tenses
• Describing costumes and film characters • Information exchange: describing actions, agreeing a sequence • Preparing and presenting an action scene	Costumes Film making	Passive forms contd Revision of Level 2 language base

Older relatives

A

◄1 Listening puzzle. Four students describe their older relatives. Listen and match each speaker with one or two photos.

B

C

D

E

F

G

Brita Picture(s): _____

Key words: _____

Simona Picture(s): _____

Key words: _____

Lee Picture(s): _____

Key words: _____

Arturo Picture(s): _____

Key words: _____

Which key words did you use to choose the photos? Write them down. Compare your choices with a partner. Then listen again and check your answers.

◄2 Vocabulary work / describing appearance. Think of an older relative or friend. Write down a few key words to help you describe their appearance.

Hair? _____

Tall or short? _____

Thin or plump? _____

Glasses? _____

Other details? _____

Now join three other students. Tell each other about your older relatives. How many key words are the same in your group?

◀**3** Before you listen, prepare your answers to these questions.

1 Do you live in the same town or village as your grandparents?
2 Have you got things that your grandparents didn't have?
3 Did your grandparents have anything that you haven't got?

▨ Study the speech bubbles. Then listen to Simona and Lee comparing their answers to the three questions. Put *L* (for Lee) or *S* (for Simona) in the speech bubbles to show the speaker.

> I use my computer a lot.

> They all lived in the same village.

> I live in the city.

> They didn't have a car.

> They didn't have a television.

> My grandparents live in the country.

> My grandparents lived in China.

◀**4** ▨ Listen to six questions about the conversation. Make notes: write down one or two key words for each question. Discuss the right answer for each question with your partner. Listen again and take turns to answer the questions.

◀**5** ▧ Look back at the questions in exercise 3 and the answers you prepared. Talk about them with your partner, then join another pair and compare your answers.

◀**6** ▧ Describing events. With a partner, take turns to describe the photos. Help each other with difficulties.

A Teaching Uncle David to skateboard

B Helping Grandpa in the kitchen

C On a bike ride with Granny

D Uncle Jim teaching me to play chess

Try to remember a time when you did something or went somewhere with an older person. Tell your partner about it. You can use these questions to help you.

Who was the older person? What did he or she look like on that day?
When was it? Was it during school time, or during your holidays? How old were you?
Where was it?
What did you and the older person do? Was it fun? Did anything unusual happen?
Was anyone else there with the two of you?

Can your teacher tell you about something they did with an older person when they were young? Ask questions.

Brothers and sisters

First Child   Middle Children   Last Child

Only Child

1 Discussing / negotiating choices. Are you a first child, a middle child, a last child or an only child? Join two or three other students in your category.

In your groups, look at the words below. Help each other with difficulties. Which words describe the people in your group? Choose three of them, or use your own words.

☐ relaxed   ☐ gentle   ☐ bossy   ☐ kind
☐ serious   ☐ fun-loving   ☐ responsible
☐ clever   ☐ rude   ☐ easily bored
☐ confident   ☐ hardworking   ☐ lazy
☐ active   ☐ lonely   ☐ spoilt   ☐ sad
☐ happy   ☐ impatient

What do you think: is a child's position in the family important, or not?

2 Listening for specific items. You are going to hear a radio presenter, Isabella Vane, interviewing a psychologist, Dr Glover. They use some of the words above. Who do they describe? Put *F* for a first child, *M* for middle children, *L* for a last child, or *O* for an only child.

Check your answers with other students. Then listen again and check that you understand Dr Glover's opinions.

3 In a small group, discuss these questions:

1 Does Dr Glover think the child's position in the family is important? Is he sure?
2 Does Isabella think his opinions are true for him?
3 Does Isabella think his opinions are true for her?
4 Do Dr Glover's descriptions match with the words you chose for your group in exercise 1?
5 Are his opinions true for you, or for your brothers or sisters?

4 Listening for gist. Listen to four students answering an interviewer's question. Which question do you think she asked them?

a How many brothers and sisters have you got?
b What do you like about your brothers and sisters?
c Is there anything that annoys you about your brothers or sisters?

10

◀**5** 📟 Now listen to the whole interview. This time, you'll hear the interviewer's question at the beginning. Check your answer to exercise 4. Continue listening, and match each student with the right family.

A

B

C

D

E

1 Lauren

2 Nicholas

3 John

4 Yusuf

5 Betty

◀**6** Work in pairs. Can you remember which student:

- [ ] gets on very well with his sisters?
- [ ] has got a twin brother?
- [ ] finds bits of cake all over his bed?
- [ ] has got a lot of friends?
- [ ] argues all the time?
- [ ] has a sister who takes his things?
- [ ] hates it when her brother watches football?

📟 Listen again and check your answers. Then, with your partner, try to remember two extra details from the interview. Compare your extra details with other students in your class.

◀**7** 〰 Role-play. You are going to prepare a 'radio interview'.

- Think of your own answers to these questions.

  If you've got brothers and sisters: What do you like about your brothers or sisters? Is there anything which annoys you about them?

  If you're an only child: What do you like about being an only child? Is there anything you don't like?

- **Work in a group of four and prepare your radio interview. One of you is the interviewer.**

  Interviewer: You are going to ask the other students questions about their families. With their help, prepare two or three questions.

  Other students: You are going to answer the interviewer's questions about your families. Use the ideas you prepared at the beginning of this exercise. Help each other find good expressions.

- Perform your interview for another group or the class. If you can, record your interview and play the tape to the class, as a radio interview.

11

In Dublin's fair city

◁**1** Listening for gist. Listen to the beginning of an interview with Maggie and choose the right answers to the questions.

1 What is Maggie's job?
   a a hotel receptionist
   b a travel agent
   c a tour guide
2 What is she talking about?
   a where to eat in Dublin
   b what to see in Dublin
   c where to stay in Dublin

◁**2** Predicting. Before you listen to the rest of the interview, which of these expressions do you expect to hear in it? With a partner, choose five of them.

the beach   an interesting building   a farm
an aeroplane   old buildings and courtyards
a table   a beautiful 18th century square
a statue   a telephone   a lovely park

◁**3** Listening for specific items. Listen and check your guesses in exercise 2. Maggie does not mention two of the Dublin tourist attractions in these photos. Which ones? Listen again if necessary.

the Bank of Ireland

the Post Office

the National Gallery

the castle

St Stephen's Green

the statue of Molly Malone

Merrion Square

Trinity College, Dublin

◄**4** 📼 Listen again. This time, follow the route Maggie takes with her groups. Add the names of the two missing buildings.

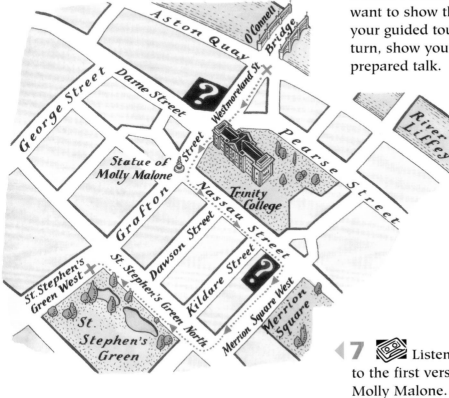

◄**5** 👄 Work in pairs. How does Maggie describe her walking tour? Use the map, and the prompts below. Take turns to say it to each other.

1 We start at …
2 On the right side, there's …
3 Just across the street, opposite the Bank, is …
4 On the corner of Grafton Street and Nassau Street, there's …
5 Then we usually walk along Nassau Street until …
6 On one side of that corner is …
7 And on the other side …
8 We turn left and into …

◄**6** 👄 Imagine that you are taking some visitors around the city, town or village where you live. With your partner, draw a simple street map of one interesting part. Decide on three or four things that you want to show the visitors. Prepare a talk for your guided tour. Then join another pair. In turn, show your map and give your prepared talk.

◄**7** 📼 Listening for specific items. Listen to the first verse of the famous song about Molly Malone.

1 Which of these things does she sell?

  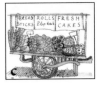

2 What does the singer think about the girls in Dublin?
   a They're clever.   **b** They're strong.
   c They're pretty.
3 What word in the song gives the opposite of a *wide* (or *broad*) street?
   a slim   **b** narrow   **c** thin

Listen to the whole song. You can find the words on page 64. Sing along if you like!

Show me round!

◀**1** Vocabulary work. What can visitors do
in your town or city? With a partner, put the
expressions in the box under one of the
headings. Add at least one other expression
to each list.

Visitors can: Visitors can't:

go swimming   go skiing play tennis   play golf go on a bus tour of the city
visit an art gallery   visit a science museum   visit a museum of history
visit an interesting building (name it)   visit a palace or castle
go shopping in a shopping centre   visit an outdoor market   relax in a park
go to the theatre   go to the cinema   have lunch in a restaurant
go to a disco   have a drink in a café   go on a boat   walk over a bridge

Compare your columns with another pair.

◀**2** Listen to some students playing a
chain game, using their lists. With a partner,
choose verbs from the box below to complete
the rules of the game.

1 Student A _____ an expression from
   either column and _____ a short
   sentence with it.
2 Student B _____ the sentence and
   _____ a detail.
3 Student C _____ a new detail, and so on.
4 Try to _____ for as long as possible.
   Your group _____ one point for each
   student who adds to the sentence.

adds   continue   makes   gets   repeats
adds   chooses

◀**3** Play the chain game, using your lists.

◄**4** With a partner, find these places on the map:

MOMI ☐   Big Ben ☐   Chelsea ☐
London Bridge ☐   Canary Wharf ☐
St Paul's ☐   Greenwich ☐
the Mountaintop Ski Village ☐

▨ Listen to an interview with another tour guide, Peter. Number the places as you hear them: 1 for the first you hear, 2 for the second, and so on. The last attraction Peter mentions is not on the map. What is it?

◄**5** Word equivalences. Can you remember the expressions Peter or the interviewer used to say these things? The words you need are all in the box.

1 *the things that tourists always want to see in a place:* _____ attractions
2 *a boat that takes tourists along the river:* a _____
3 *You can't be serious!:* You must _____
4 *a place to ski which doesn't use snow:* an _____ slope

| ski   riverbus   tourist   be   artificial |
| joking   traditional |

▨ Now listen again to the interview and complete or check your answers.

◄**6** 👄 Information exchange.

Student A: Look at page 56.
Student B: Look at page 60.

Shampoo Blues (1)

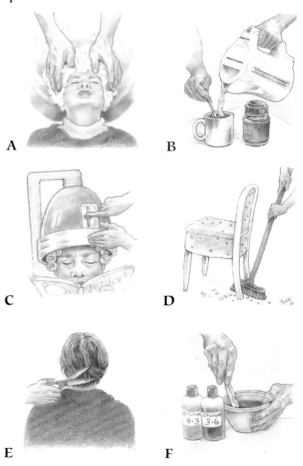

WEDNESDAY PM

Thirty Minute Theatre
Shampoo Blues *by Carmen Chanebury*

Cast: *1 The Hairdressers*
Ray, the owner   Jim Still
Eva, the assistant Angela Elek
Ronnie, stylist   Rod Kemp
2 The Customers
Mrs Warner   Jean Plathy
Grant   Phil Spiney
Helen   Joan Bradford

◀1 Listening for gist. Listen to an announcement once and choose the right answer to question 1.

1 What is the announcement about?
   a a radio concert
   b a radio play
   c a radio sports programme

Listening for specific items. Read questions 2, 3 and 4. Then listen again and choose the right answers.

2 Where does Eva come from?
   a Romania   **b** Russia   **c** Austria

3 How is she finding her life in the hairdressing salon?
   a She doesn't like it.
   b She's finding it strange.
   c She's getting on very well.

4 What are the two possible things that can happen to Eva?
   a She can earn a lot of money or she can be very poor.
   b She can travel a lot or she can stay in England.
   c She can keep her job or she can lose her job because of angry customers.

Check your answers with other students.

◀2 Listen to the beginning of episode 1. Which of the characters do we hear? Which actions do they mention? Tick three pictures.

A

B

C

D

E

F

16

◀ **3** 🔊 Listen to the next part of episode 1. Use one word from the box to complete each sentence. Together, the sentences are a summary of the action.

Eva went to the kitchen to make some _____. Ronnie came to see if she wanted any _____. Ronnie and Eva heard a _____. Mrs Warner was very angry because her _____ was burnt. Eva poured coffee over _____. Ronnie used a towel to clean Grant's _____. Ronnie went to get another _____ for Grant.

Grant	hair	coffee	scream	coffee
jacket	help			

With a partner, read your summaries to each other and compare them.

◀ **4** 🔊 Asking for repetition. Study the expressions in the box. Listen again. Which of these expressions does Ronnie tell Eva to use when she doesn't understand?

Repeat.
Pardon me?
I'm sorry, but I don't understand.
I beg your pardon?
Sorry?
Could you repeat that, please?
Would you mind repeating that?
Please say that again.

Why does Ronnie tell Eva to use these expressions?

◀ **5** 🔊 Listen to the end of episode 1. Decide if the following sentences are *true* (✓) or *false* (✗).

1 Helen was angry because her hair was brown, not red. ☐

2 Ray didn't like the new colour on Helen. ☐

3 Ronnie prepared some new colour for Helen. ☐

4 Ray found the tapes and put on some music. ☐

Check your answers with other students.

◀ **6** 🔊 People express their anger through intonation. Listen carefully to the intonation patterns in the following sentences from episode 1. If the sentences express anger, raise your right hand. If the sentences don't express anger, raise your left hand.

◀ **7** 🗣 Retelling a story. In groups of four, retell the story of *Shampoo Blues* in turn. Use the past simple. Try to remember all the details.

◀ **8** 🗣 Predicting / discussing. In your group, talk about these questions:

What do you think happens next in the story?
Does Eva lose her job?
How can she try to improve her English so that she doesn't make mistakes?

Shampoo Blues (2)

◄**1**  Before you listen. Episode 2 of *Shampoo Blues* begins with an introduction, then a short summary of episode 1 for listeners who didn't hear the first part. With a partner, prepare the summary by completing this text.

Introduction
We present episode 2 of Shampoo Blues, a play by Carmen Chanebury, starring Angela Elek and Rod Kemp.

Summary of episode 1
In episode 1, Eva, a young Romanian hairdressing assistant, couldn't understand instructions from

the owner, Ray

She burnt one customer's

hair

She turned another customer's hair red instead of

blonde

She poured oil

the coffee over the colour

And if that wasn't enough, Ray couldn't find the

tapes

Setting the scene for episode 2
In episode 2 it's now the next morning, and Eva and Ronnie, the stylist, are alone in the kitchen of the hairdressing salon . . .

Join another pair. In turn, say your introductions and compare them.

◄**2**  Listen to the play's introduction. In your group of four, compare your introductions with the play's.

18

◀ 3 Listen to the first part of episode 2 and answer the questions.

1 Who took the tapes? Why?
2 What did Ray tell Eva to do?
3 What did Eva do?

Check your answers with other students.

◀ 4 Guessing meaning from context. Listen again and match the phrases in list A with expressions from the play in list B.

A	B
very angry	upset
quite angry or irritated	get the sack
very unhappy	furious
lose a job	annoyed
a terrible situation	a mess

Check your answers with other students.

◀ 5 Discussing possibilities. In a small group, discuss these questions and come to a decision about what is best for the characters to do.

What's the best thing for Ronnie to do now?
What's the best thing for Eva to do now?

Compare your ideas with those of other groups. Write possible actions for the three characters on the board.

◀ 6 Listen to the final part of episode 2. What did Ronnie decide to do? Was he successful?

◀ 7 Creating and narrating a sequence of events. How do you think the story ended? Work with a partner. Use the ideas below, or think of your own. Write down some key words or a few sentences to help you. Then tell the class your ending.

> Ronnie lost his job.
>
> Ronnie thought of a good excuse, and Ray believed him.
>
> Eva explained her misunderstanding.
>
> Ray forgave Eva but said she couldn't work there anymore.
>
> Eva went back to Romania.
>
> Ray said Eva could stay, but only if Ronnie supervised her very closely and helped her with her English.
>
> Ronnie and Eva became very close friends.

Flying high

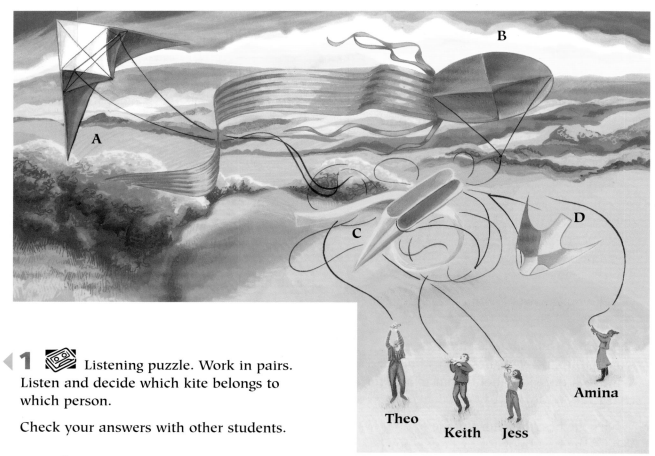

1 Listening puzzle. Work in pairs. Listen and decide which kite belongs to which person.

Check your answers with other students.

2 Identifying the mood of speakers. Listen to the four teenagers talking about kite flying.

Student A: Make notes on the two boys.   Student B: Make notes on the two girls.

	has positive views	is uncertain	likes it because . .	is uncertain because . .
Theo				
Jess				
Keith				
Amina				

Compare notes with your partner and talk about the views expressed. Have you got any experience of kite flying?

◀ **3** 📟 Vocabulary work. Work with a partner. Listen again and pick out:

Expressions that show enthusiasm: _____

Expressions that show uncertainty: _____

Expressions that show dislike: _____

Check your answers with other students.

◀ **4** 👄 Expressing certainty, uncertainty, enthusiasm, dislike.

- Choose an activity (or a sport) that you enjoy doing. What's good about it? What's difficult or not so good?

- Work in a group of four. One of you is the interviewer. Study the example, then prepare an 'interview'. Help each other to find good expressions for it.

  Interviewer: Ask the others about their activity. Ask each person at least two questions.

  Other students: Answer the questions. Use some of the expressions from exercise 3.

- Perform your interviews for another group or for the class.

Katrina, tell us about an activity that you like doing.

I really like swimming. It's fun and it's very good for you.

Is there anything that's not so good about it?

Well, I'm not so sure about some of the swimming pools around here. They're sometimes dirty, and the changing rooms are cold.

◀ **5** 👄 Information exchange.

Student A: Look at page 57.
Student B: Look at page 61.

21

Fit for life

1 Vocabulary work. What does 'being fit' mean to you? Which of these things do you think the expression can mean?

being strong   having a lot of energy
being healthy   playing sports easily
running without getting tired
moving easily   being the right weight (not too thin or too fat)

Compare your ideas with other students.

2 Before you listen. Look at the activities below. Which ones do you think can improve fitness? Compare your ideas with other students.

3 Listen to an expert discussing the eight activities. He explains what is good about them, and what is not good. Complete the notes below. Check your answers with a partner.

4 With your partner, can you remember which sports these are?

1 It's becoming popular, especially with women.
2 It's a very natural exercise.
3 All children are now learning it at school.
4 They're becoming popular with both young and old.
5 Take care when you do these two activities.

 Listen again and check your answers.

D *Jogging, running:*
    + _____
    – *can have injuries to legs and* _____

E *Exercise classes, dance:*
    + *good all-round exercise, especially for* _____

A *Walking:*
    + *good for* _____
    – *doesn't make you* _____

F *Racket sports:*
    + *good for all-round* _____, *help you* _____

B *Swimming:*
    + *improves energy, makes you* _____, *good for general* _____

G *Weight training:*
    + *you get* _____, *proper training is very* _____

C *Cycling:*
    + *good for* _____, *makes legs strong*
    – *pollution and traffic* _____

H *Team games:*
    + *good for* _____, *make you strong, help you* _____
    – *risk of getting* _____, *so* _____ *is very important*

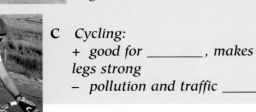

◄**5** 👄 Requesting and displaying information. How many students in your class participate in these activities? Organise a class survey and put a bar chart on the board. Chart A is an example.

📼 Now listen to the expert giving the percentage of young people in Britain who participate in the activities. Complete chart B.

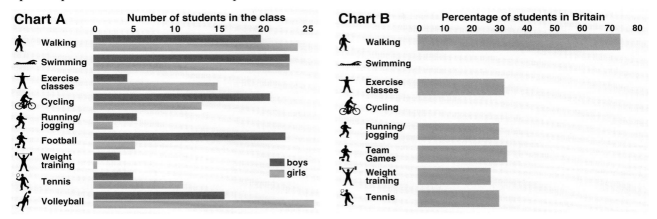

◄**6** 📼 Expressing plans and intentions. Listen to three people talking about their plans for getting fit. Complete the grid. Use the activities in the box to help you.

| running | soccer | tennis | weight training | swimming | jogging |
| no exercises | cycling | walking | | | |

	What they are doing now	What they plan to do
Speaker 1		
Speaker 2		
Speaker 3		

◄**7** 👄 Work with two partners. Take it in turns to describe what each speaker is doing now, and what they're going to do.

◄**8** 👄 Do you think you are fit now? If you are fit, what are you going to do to keep fit? If you are not fit, what are you going to do to get fit? Talk about it with other students. How many of you have definite plans for getting fit or keeping fit?

Unit 5. The best sequence for you to follow the whole story in Unit 5 is:

1 Listening and Speaking book, Lesson 5A
2 Reading and Writing book, Lesson 5A
3 Listening and Speaking book, Lesson 5B
4 Reading and Writing book, Lesson 5B

Strange signals

◀ **1** Listen and choose the right answers.

1 What situation do you hear?
   a a shop assistant talking to a customer
   b a scientist talking to another scientist in a laboratory
   c a radio presenter interviewing a scientist

2 What emotion does the man express?
   a anger   **b** no interest   **c** surprise

Check your answers with other students.

◀ **2** Predicting / discussing. With a partner, discuss the radio signals. Do you think they come from other people on the new planet? Do you think the other people are friendly? What do you think is the best thing to do about the signals?

◀ **3** Listen to four scientists meeting to decide what to do about the radio signals. Find the right opinion (or opinions) for each scientist from the box.

Dr White: _____

Dr Huber: _____

Dr Costello: _____

Dr Lee: _____

find out more about the planet
do nothing   act straight away   just wait
start planning a mission immediately
protect ourselves   send a spaceship
send a team of scientists

◀ **4** Vocabulary work. Can you remember any of the expressions used for these situations? Check with other students.

Asking for a person's views: _____

Disagreeing politely with a person's

views: _____

Agreeing with a person's views: _____

Listen again and add expressions to your list.

◀ **5** 🗪 Negotiating / reporting decisions. In a small group, discuss the problem, and the four views. What is the best thing to do, in your opinion? Prepare a short oral report of your group's choice. Give at least two reasons for your decision. Report to the class. Are the choices in your class similar or different?

◀ **6** 📼 Listen and compare your choice with the committee's decision.

◀ **7** 🗪 Imagine that your group must choose a captain to be the leader of the mission to Wonstonia. Look at the qualities in the box. Choose two or three that you think are the most important for a leader.

> gets on well with other people
> is firm, keeps discipline   is imaginative
> thinks quickly in emergencies
> is experienced   is calm, doesn't panic
> knows a lot about space missions
> is confident

◀ **8** 📼 Now listen to Gaby Huber interviewing Dr Wells, the person she chooses as captain of the mission. Tick the qualities in the box that you think Dr Wells has.

Check your answers with other students. Do you think Dr Wells will be a good captain?

◀ **9** 🗪 Discussing / predicting. Do you think there will be any problems on the mission to Wonstonia? What do you think the team will find on the new planet? Compare your views with other students in the class.

NAME: Patricia Wells
STATUS: Single
AGE : 36
PREVIOUS EXPERIENCE: Captain Venusian space mission; 2 years ; Senior Flight Officer, Lunar probe, 26 months A   Space

Will they get back?

A On board the spaceship

B Earth Station 540 trying to make contact with Ranger

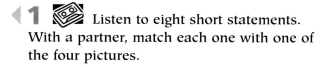 **1** Listen to eight short statements. With a partner, match each one with one of the four pictures.

Check your answers with other students.

2 Listening for gist. Listen to the complete situations. Take notes and discuss the story with another student.

3 Listen to six statements. Which of them can you say *for sure* are either *true* or *false*?

C Television journalists reporting the events

	True	False	We can't tell.
1			
2			
3			
4			
5			
6			

D Dr Costello talking to a team member's wife

Check your answers with a partner.
Give reasons for your choices.

◀ **4** Role-play. With a partner, prepare an improvised dialogue. Choose one of the two situations and prepare a short dialogue.

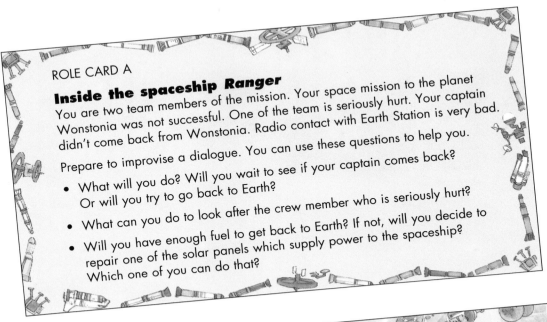

ROLE CARD A

Inside the spaceship *Ranger*

You are two team members of the mission. Your space mission to the planet Wonstonia was not successful. One of the team is seriously hurt. Your captain didn't come back from Wonstonia. Radio contact with Earth Station is very bad.

Prepare to improvise a dialogue. You can use these questions to help you.

• What will you do? Will you wait to see if your captain comes back? Or will you try to go back to Earth?

• What can you do to look after the crew member who is seriously hurt?

• Will you have enough fuel to get back to Earth? If not, will you decide to repair one of the solar panels which supply power to the spaceship? Which one of you can do that?

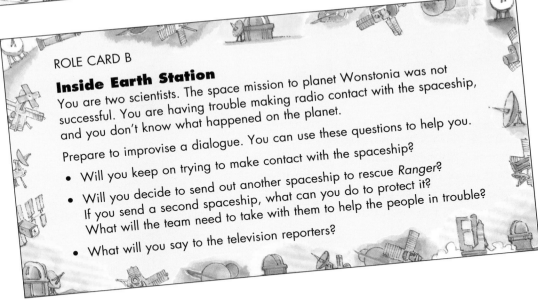

ROLE CARD B

Inside Earth Station

You are two scientists. The space mission to planet Wonstonia was not successful. You are having trouble making radio contact with the spaceship, and you don't know what happened on the planet.

Prepare to improvise a dialogue. You can use these questions to help you.

• Will you keep on trying to make contact with the spaceship?

• Will you decide to send out another spaceship to rescue *Ranger*? If you send a second spaceship, what can you do to protect it? What will the team need to take with them to help the people in trouble?

• What will you say to the television reporters?

◀ **5** Present your improvised dialogue to another pair, or to the class. Then talk about the story ending. Do you think it will be a happy ending, a sad ending or a mysterious ending?

Stranger than fiction

1  With a partner, look at the five pictures. Choose one and together make up a short story of a few sentences about what happened next. Use past tenses. Join another pair. Tell each other your stories.

Example:

> This is a story about a fisherman. He was sitting by the side of a river.

> But he didn't catch any fish that day, so he decided to …

2 Listen to eight sentences. With a partner, decide which picture each sentence could go with.

◁**3** 📼 Listening for gist. Listen to a conversation and answer the questions.

1 What is it about?
   a strange statuettes on a shelf
   b a car accident that really happened
   c strange things that really happened

2 Which two pictures on page 28 go with these stories?

Compare your reaction to these true stories with other students. Does anyone have a strange but true story to tell the class?

◁**4** Vocabulary work. In the conversation, the speakers sometimes used two or more expressions with similar meanings. With a partner, match the phrases in list A with one or more expressions in list B.

A	B
strange	chunky
not what you'd call slim	creepy
hotel	terrified
ornaments	weird
scared	china statuettes
	inn
	fairly heavy

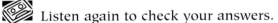 Listen again to check your answers.

◁**5** 📼 Listening for gist. A group of students are going to play a panel game. Listen to the teacher introducing the game and answer the questions.

1 What are the rules of the game?
2 Anthea, Jemima and Paolo are going to tell stories, but in what order?

📼 Listening and making notes. Work in a group of three. Student A makes notes on the first story, Student B on the second, Student C on the third. Decide before you start who is A, B and C, then listen to the stories.

◁**6** 👄 Narrating events in the past / negotiating choices. Retell your story to your partners. In your group, decide which you think is the true story. Give a reason for your choice.

◁**7** 📼 Listening for confirmation. Listen to the end of the game. How many of you guessed the right answer?

◁**8** 👄 Organize a panel game in your class. Two or three panels prepare stories. Play the game in your next class.

Weird and wonderful

1 Vocabulary work: idiomatic language. With a partner, match the expressions in list A with the correct definition in list B. Check your answers with other students.

A

to work through a lunch hour
to catch up with some work
to get something back
to accept a cheque

B

to receive a bank cheque as payment, instead of cash
to work during the time when you usually eat
to do extra work to finish all the things that you need to do
to receive something that you lost

2  Listen to a news report. Number the pictures to show the right order.

A

B

C

D

E

◀ **3** You are going to hear a second news story in sections. Work in pairs.

- Listen to the beginning of the second news story – until the musical signal. When did the story happen to Mr and Mrs Murray? Which picture shows what happens next?

A

B

C

- Listen to the next part of the story. Which was the right picture? With your partner, guess what happens next.

- Listen to the next part of the story. With your partner, discuss Mr and Mrs Murray's problem. What is the best thing for them to do?

- Listen to the next part of the story. What did Mr and Mrs Murray decide? What do you think the mistake was?

- Listen to the end of the story. What did the robbers do? Why was it a mistake?

◀ **4** Listening for detail. How much do you remember about the two news items? Listen to two statements about each story. They are wrong. With your partner, correct each statement.

◀ **5** With your partner, prepare one more false sentence about each story. Join another pair. In turn, tell each other your two sentences and see if the others can correct them.

◀ **6** Information exchange.

Student A: Look at page 57.
Student B: Look at page 61.

Unit 7
A
Bright and colourful

◀ **1**  Before you listen. Work in pairs. Put your hands on your desk, palms down. Compare your hands. Consider these questions.

1 Which of you has: bigger hands? longer fingers? thinner fingers? a shorter thumb?
2 Is either of you wearing: a ring or rings? a bracelet or bracelets? a watch?
3 If you are both wearing a watch, which is: bigger? newer? brighter or more colourful?

Together, prepare two sentences to summarize your observations. Join another pair and share your comparisons.

1 Which person in your group has the: biggest hands? longest fingers? thinnest fingers? shortest thumb?
2 Who is wearing: the biggest watch? the newest watch? the brightest or most colourful watch or jewellery?

◀ **2** Predicting. You are going to hear an advertisement for the jewellery counter in a department store. Which of these expressions do you expect to hear? Check any difficult meanings with other students or with your teacher.

kites   watches   story book   cassette   stop-watch   traditional styles
widest selection   tennis balls   bracelets   rings   gift problems

Listen and check your guesses. Were there any surprises?

◀ **3** Listening for specific items. Listen again. What does the advertisement suggest as gifts for these people.

Younger members of the family: _____

_____

Sporty teenagers: _____

Parents: _____

Special friends: _____

Check your answers with other students.

◀ **4** Listen to Brenda choosing gifts at the jewellery counter and answer the questions.

1 Which of the items in the picture are mentioned by the salesman?
2 Who is Brenda choosing gifts for?
3 What does she choose?
4 What do you think of her choice?

◀ **5** 🖭 Listen again and fill in the comparatives and superlatives in these sentences.

1 The black and green watch is the _____ watch in the shop.

2 The cat watch is _____ than the black and green one.

3 The watch with the red strap is _____ and _____ than the cat watch.

4 The bracelets are _____ than the watches.

◀ **6** 👄 Do this by yourself. Imagine that you are at the jewellery counter. Think of a good present for your partner, and one for the teacher. Think of a reason for your choices.

When you are ready, join your partner. Tell each other about your choices and the reasons for them. Are you happy with your partner's choice of a watch for you?

Tell the teacher which watch you chose and ask for his/her reaction.

Comfortable and stylish

◀**3** Listen to three short advertisements. Match the adjectives in the box with the right picture.

completely waterproof   the most stylish
the safest   less expensive   the best
different   the most comfortable
the most modern   cool

A Nova all-weather walking boots

_____

_____

_____

◀**1** Listening to and carrying out instructions. Study the drawing. Then listen and follow the instructions.

◀**2** Vocabulary work. With a partner, make sure you understand these adjectives.

light   warm   soft   waterproof   durable
safe   stylish   luxurious

Which of the adjectives can go with these things?

boots   sandals   Doc Marten shoes
a jacket   a hat   earrings   a watch
a cycling helmet

Compare your ideas with other students.

B The sports sandal
that thinks it's a trainer

_____
_____
_____

C Doc Martens
– still the most stylish

_____
_____
_____

4 🗨 With a partner, prepare an advertisement like the ones you heard, for a pair of shoes one of you is wearing today. Use some of the adjectives from the previous exercises. Remember that advertisements use lots of comparatives and superlatives. Take turns saying the advertisement. When you are ready, join another pair and compare your advertisements.

5 🗨 Discussing / negotiating. Sit in a small groups of three or four people. Discuss your shoes, and other accessories (an accessory is anything extra that people wear, in addition to their clothes – for example watches, other types of jewellery, bags, hats, etc.).
Who has …

… the most comfortable pair of shoes?
… the most stylish pair of shoes?
… the most interesting accessory?
… the oldest accessory?
… the funniest or most delightful accessory?
… the most colourful accessory?

How important do you think accessories are? Do you think they say something about the kind of person you are? Are they more important to you or less important to you than your basic clothes?

Compare your ideas with others in your class.

Travel tales

A ☐

E ☐

F ☐

◄1 Listen to eight questions. You will hear two questions, then a musical signal. When you hear the musical signal, match each question you've just heard with a picture.

Listen again and write down one or two key words for each picture. Check your answers with a partner.

◄2 Using the pictures and your key words, take it in turns to ask your partner the eight questions. If your partner answers 'Yes, I have', ask a follow-on question.

Example:

A: Have you ever had a holiday on a boat?
B: No, I haven't.
A: Have you ever been on holiday to a very hot place?
B: Yes, I have.
A: Where was that?
B: We went to Egypt in the summer. It was very hot.

◄3 Before you listen / vocabulary work. Look at these verbs. With a partner, discuss their meanings. Can you translate them? Ask others or use a dictionary if you need help.

book (a hotel)	pretend
moan (in pain)	groan

Listening for gist. Listen to two people talking. What is the conversation about?

a horrible experiences on holiday
b happy experiences on holiday
c funny experiences on holiday

◄4 Vocabulary work. Look at the phrases in the box. Put each one into one of these two categories:

Phrases that express sympathy with the speaker/speaker's story: _____
_____

Phrases that help the speaker to continue telling a story: _____
_____

> What did you do?   Was he all right?
> What bad luck!   Oh, how awful!
> What happened?

Narrating / reacting. Work in pairs. Each person retells one story.

Speaker: Imagine that you had the horrible experience. Use the pronoun 'I'.

Listener: Help your partner by reacting and asking questions.

B ☐ C ☐ D ☐ G ☐ H ☐

◀**5** Use one of these sentence beginnings. Write a complete sentence on a slip of paper. *Don't* show it to anybody!

*The most interesting thing
I ever did on holiday was …*

*The most unusual holiday
I ever had was …*

*The funniest thing that ever
happened to me on holiday was …*

*The most boring holiday
I ever had was …*

*The most horrible time I
ever had on holiday was …*

Your teacher will collect all the slips of paper.

◀**6** Listening for specific items. Listen to a class playing a game with similar slips of paper. The teacher has given one group of four students four slips from a different group. Tick (✓) the right answers.

	Tom	Jennifer	Claudia	Bill	We don't know.
1 Who has had a holiday in a caravan?					
2 Who has been on a camping holiday?					
3 Who didn't do anything last summer?					
4 Who has tried scuba diving?					

◀**7** Sit in a group of four. Your teacher will give you four slips of paper. In your group, guess who wrote the four slips. Discuss your guesses, then write them down. You get one point for each correct guess.

The high road

◀ **1** Before you listen. Have you ever been to Scotland? How much do you know about it? Which of these pictures show Scottish things or places? Check your answers with other students.

◀ **2** Listen to a travel agent, and check your answers.

◀ **3** Vocabulary work. The travel agent uses many adjectives to describe Scotland. Match the adjectives in list A with the nouns in list B.

	A	B
1	dramatic	villages
2	picturesque	piper
3	shining	interest
4	beautiful	lochs
5	mysterious	mountains
6	capital	Edinburgh Festival
7	historical	city
8	spectacular	lakes
9	colourful	Loch Ness monster

Check your answers with other students, then listen again for confirmation if you wish.

1

2

3

7

4

5

6

8

9

◀ **4** 📼 A teacher has brought her school group to visit Edinburgh, but some problems have come up. Listen and write the problem under each picture. Make a note about the solution.

Check your answers with other students.

B Problem: The travel agent hasn't …
Solution: …

A Problem: The hotel has …
Solution: …

C Problem: The ticket agent hasn't …
Solution: …

◀ **5** Making apologies. You've just heard three people apologizing. Which of these expressions did they use?

> Please accept my apology.
> I'm terribly sorry.
> There's nothing I can do about it.
> I'm sorry about that.
> I must apologize.
> It's not my fault, you know.
> I'm really very sorry.

📼 Listen again to check your answers.

◀ **6** 👄 Information exchange.

Student A: Look at page 58.
Student B: Look at page 62.

◀ **7** 📼 Listen to the song which the folk singer performs especially for the group. Answer the questions.

1 Have the two lovers in the song just met, or just separated?
2 What are the two ways of going to Scotland in the song?

Listen again and sing along if you like. You can find the words on page 64.

39

Sweet tooth

1 ☐ jelly beans
2 ☐ chocolates
3 ☐ chocolate bar
4 ☐ toffees
5 ☐ mints
6 ☐ licorice
7 ☐ cake
8 ☐ biscuits
9 ☐ ice cream
10 ☐ ice lolly

My favourites:

_____

_____

◁ 1  Before you listen. Are your favourite sweet things in the picture? Add your favourites.

Work in pairs and answer these questions.

Which of the sweets do you like now? Are there any you dislike?

Have you eaten any of them since the beginning of this week? Are there any that you've never eaten?

Do you eat more sweets (or fewer sweets) now than you did when you were six years old?

◁ 2 ▨ Listening for specific items. Listen to a conversation. Tick the sweet things that are mentioned. Then listen again and answer the questions.

1 Are the speakers children?
2 Which of the speakers has stopped eating sweet things? Why or why not?
3 What does the word *filling* mean? (Use the context to help you.)

◁ 3 ▨ Vocabulary work: using context to understand meaning. Listen to three sentences that the speakers use. Choose the sentence that is closest in meaning.

1 a I remembered my childhood.
  b I forgot my childhood.
  c I really liked my childhood.
2 a I now have a lot more fillings in my teeth than I did as a child.
  b I haven't had any fillings in my teeth recently.
  c I have stronger teeth now than I did as a child.
3 a I love chocolate now, but I didn't as a child.
  b I've always loved chocolate and I still do.
  c I haven't eaten chocolate since I was a child.

Check your answers with a partner, and compare your views. Do you have a passion for some food or sweet thing?

◀ **4** Predicting. You are going to hear a journalist talking about *sugar consumption* (how much sugar people eat) in Britain. In pairs, decide which of these points you expect the journalist to make.

1 Sugar consumption in Britain has gone down since 1900.
2 British people eat too much sugar.
3 Sugar gets into all kinds of food, including drinks.
4 There isn't any sugar in tinned foods.
5 You've probably eaten more sugar than you think since you got up this morning.

The journalist uses eight of these words. Which ones, do you think?

village   sweet   savoury   ingredient
mountains   average   bagpipes   festivals
cheeseburgers   sausages   city   lakes
kilos   grams

 Listen and check your answers.

◀ **5** Read the sentence beginnings. Then listen again. Complete the sentences so that the meaning is the same as on the tape. (You don't need to use exactly the same words.)

Student A: Complete sentences 1 and 3.
Student B: Complete sentences 2 and 4.

1 Since about 1900, sugar consumption in Europe has …
2 In Britain, each person eats …
3 The trouble is that sugar …
4 Drinks are …

Compare answers. Then listen again. This time, check your partner's two sentences. Add new details if you can.

◀ **6**  Listen to four questions and write your own answers on a piece of paper. The pictures show you key words for each question.

◀ **7** Asking questions / discussing. Work in pairs. Don't show each other your answers from exercise 6. Ask each other the questions and write down your partner's answers. Then compare your answers with others in the class. Do you think that people in your class eat too much sugar? How can you cut down on sugar?

School meals

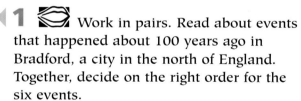

cheese and vegetable pie ☐

jelly ☐

fishcakes ☐

bread and jam ☐

vegetable soup ☐

brown bread ☐

burgers ☐

◀1 🗩 Work in pairs. Read about events that happened about 100 years ago in Bradford, a city in the north of England. Together, decide on the right order for the six events.

a The government changed the law and let them give the children free meals.
b A headmaster called W H Sykes saw that his pupils were very, very hungry.
c The government told the leaders of the town to stop giving children free meals.
d The town decided to give all its children free school meals.
e He bought food for the children.
f The people of Bradford organised a national campaign against the government.

◀2 🗎 Listen to the story and check your answers. Listen again. Add the years beside three of the sentences in the previous column.

1 1887
2 1902
3 1907

Now look at the picture and put *P* beside the foods that children had in the past. Put *N* beside the foods that children have now.

◀**3** 📼 Listening puzzle. Listen to two students talking about school meals. Fill in the missing words. The first letter of each word spells the speaker's name.

Speaker 1

> I think school _____ are a good idea. Our school food's pretty good.
> It's _____ a lot since I came here. There's _____ some choice.

> They're OK for young _____ I guess. I haven't _____ a school meal for years. It's your own choice _____, isn't it?

Speaker 2

◀**4** 📼 Listen to the two students again. With a partner, identify what arguments they have for or against school meals.

```
FOR:
_____
_____
_____

AGAINST:
_____
_____
_____
```

Check your answers with another pair.

◀**5** 👄 Exchanging views.

- With a partner, discuss the arguments you've just heard and the following questions.

1 Do you have school meals? What do you think about them?
2 Are they good for: younger children? students of your age? Why or why not?
3 Do school meals give students more chance to be together and feel that they are part of a 'team' at school?
4 Is it important for the school to know where students are over the lunch period?
5 Are school meals too expensive?
6 Can you add any other arguments for or against school meals?

- Reporting views. Join another pair and discuss your ideas. Help one person in your group to prepare a short report (two or three sentences) about your discussion.

- Report your discussion to the class.

Protect and survive

1 Work in pairs. Match the words and the pictures.

helmet   helmet   goggles   wrist and knee protectors   lights   lifejacket   hard hat   gloves

A ☐   B ☐   C ☐   D ☐

E ☐   F ☐   G ☐   H ☐

What sports are they for? Check your answers with other students.

2 Listening for specific items. Listen to an interview with the manager of a sports shop. Tick (✓) the items he mentions.

3 Vocabulary work: using context to understand meaning. With your partner, find the expressions from the box which mean:

  a obligatory
  b a good idea
  c allow someone to do something

┌───┐
│ absolutely necessary   we recommend them   │
│   the law says people must have them   │
│ that's the law   let someone do something │
└───┘

Listen again and confirm your answers. Then, with your partner, answer these questions.

1 Which of the pieces of equipment are obligatory? Which are a good idea?
2 What can't you do in England without a helmet?
3 What can you do in England without a helmet?

A

Check your answers with other students.

4 Role-play. The pictures on the right show which pieces of equipment are obligatory, and which are not, for sailing and riding.

Role play an interview like the one you heard. Take it in turns to be the interviewer and the sports shop manager. Start this way:

Interviewer: You've got a lot of equipment to protect people who do sports here. What's absolutely necessary for people who want to go sailing?

Shop manager: Well …

Join another pair and perfom your role-plays.

Obligatory
A good idea

B

C

A good idea Obligatory

5 Listening for gist. Listen as the interview with Mr Tadiki continues. Which pictures show the two stories he talks about?

Retelling a story. Work in pairs. Listen to the interview again.

Student A: Retell the first story of survival.
Student B: Retell the second story of survival.

6 Information exchange.

Student A: Look at page 59.
Student B: Look at page 63.

Keep calm

◀1 Describing a scene of action. Look at the picture for about five minutes and prepare to describe it. Use a dictionary or ask others if you need words or expressions. Make notes.

Close your books. Play a game with other students. One person starts by giving one detail about the picture in a complete sentence. The next person adds a new detail, and so on. How long can you continue?

◀2 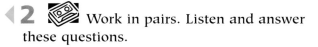 Work in pairs. Listen and answer these questions.

1 Who was the phone call from?
2 What did the caller want Mr or Mrs Sinen to do?
3 How would you describe the caller's mood: emotional? panicky? calm? reassuring? confident? worried? Can you say why?
4 What new information have you got about the situation? What do you think the problem is?

Compare your ideas with other students.

◀3 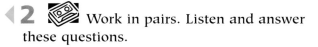 Listening for gist. Listen to a phone call. What is the problem?

Listen again. With a partner, make notes under these headings.

Expressions Mr Sinen uses that show his worry:

_____

Expressions Mrs O'Brien uses to reassure him:

_____

Join other students in a small group and compare your notes.

◀4 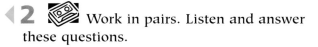 Discussion / role-play. In your small group, imagine and discuss the situation of the trapped students. Consider these questions:

What are the problems for the students? (not having enough air? getting panicky?)

How can they solve the problems? Think of as many ideas as you can.

What would you do in their situation?

Role-play. You are the trapped students. Prepare an improvised conversation as you wait for the rescue teams. Perform your conversation for other students.

◀5 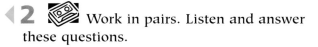 Listening and making notes. How did the students solve their problems? Listen to Denise giving an interview. Work in pairs. Student A makes notes on problem 1. Student B makes notes on problem 2. Listen a second time. Student A notes extra details for problem 2, Student B does the same for problem 1.

1 Not enough air: _____
2 Panic: _____

◀6 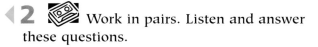 Exchanging ideas. Join your group from exercise 4, and compare what the students did, and what you imagined. Were there any similarities? Any differences? What favourite songs would you sing?

47

Treasure at sea

◀1 Listening for gist. Listen to the beginning of a radio programme and answer the questions.

1 What kind of programme is it?
2 What is this week's programme about?
3 Where is the presenter?
4 What are the divers searching for?

Check your answers with other students.

◀2 Predicting. You're going to hear more of the programme. In this part the presenter asks four questions. Match each question with the beginning of the right answer from the box below. Discuss your ideas with a partner.

1 What are you searching for, exactly?
2 Why was so much glass carried by these ships?
3 Are there shipwrecks full of glass cargoes?
4 Why are you searching in this particular area?

> **a** You see glass was very precious in those days…
> **b** Yes, sometimes the ships were caught in storms and they were wrecked…
> **c** We're looking for some old ships from Roman times…
> **d** The wreck of a Roman ship was found two years ago, just a few miles away…

◀**3** Listen and confirm your guesses in exercise 2, then listen again. Write down the way these ideas are expressed on the tape. Work in pairs.

Student A: Do 1 and 3.
Student B: Do 2 and 4.

1 Why did the ships carry so much glass? _____

2 Have you discovered records of a particular ship? _____

3 We found the wreck of a Roman ship two years ago. _____

4 Sometimes storms caught the ships. _____

Check your answers with other students.

◀**4** Do you think the *Christine Rose* divers will find a Roman ship? Listen to the next part of the programme and find out.

◀**5** This is a diagram that shows Dr Timson's emotions during her talk with the divers. Can you remember the words or expressions that express her emotions? Listen again and fill the gaps.

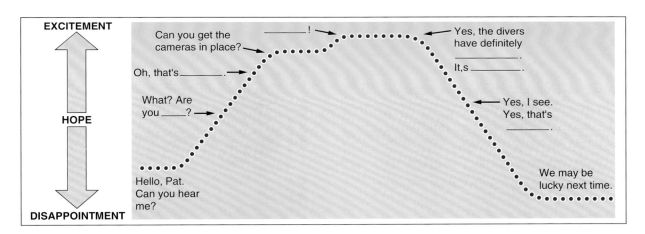

◀**6** Role-play. With your partner, prepare a news report of the day's events on board the *Christine Rose*. You can use these sentence beginnings to help you:

There were dramatic events today on board the Christine Rose, a ship which is …
A large object was located …
Two divers were sent down to …
The science team on board the ship was delighted when …
When the divers' cameras were switched on, however, …
The leader of the science team, Dr Helen Timson, said …

Present your news report to another pair or to the class.

Treasure on land

A

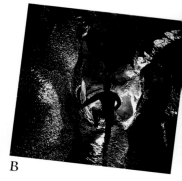

B

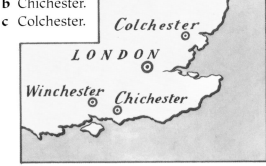

◀1 [cassette icon] Listen to the start of the following week's edition of *Science Now*. Work in pairs. Choose the right picture to illustrate the programme, and then answer the questions.

1 The programme is broadcast this week from a school near …
   a Winchester.
   b Chichester.
   c Colchester.

C

2 The search is for …
   a Roman glass.
   b some Roman coins.
   c some Roman coins and jewellery.
3 The treasure was buried by …
   a some schoolchildren in 1950.
   b some builders in 1915.
   c some treasure hunters in 1905.

Check your answers with other students.

◀2 [speech icon] Before you listen. Look at the map. The arrow marks the start of the hunt. With your partner, decide where you would start to look for the Roman treasure.

Compare your ideas with other students.

◀3 [cassette icon] Listen to the students describing their search. Did the students make the same decision as you? Listen again and follow the route that was taken by the students. Note down the times mentioned.

◀**4** 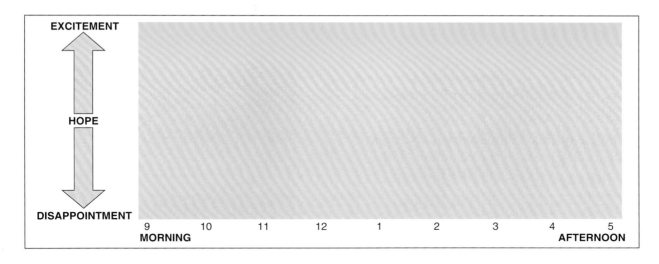 Here is a diagram to show the emotions of the students as they search for the treasure. With your partner, complete it up to 12 o'clock noon. Then decide where you would search for the treasure next.

EXCITEMENT

HOPE

DISAPPOINTMENT

| 9 | 10 | 11 | 12 | 1 | 2 | 3 | 4 | 5 |

MORNING   AFTERNOON

◀**5** Listen to the continuation of the story. Did the students make the same decision as you? With your partner, continue following their route and noting the times. Complete the emotion diagram up to 3 p.m. Then discuss the situation with your partner. What would you do? Go back to the school, like some of the students? Or continue searching? Where would you look next?

◀**6** Listen to the end of the programme. Did the students make the same decision as you? Complete the emotion diagram up to 4.30 p.m.

◀**7** Work in pairs. Look at the map and decide on a good place to bury treasure. Take turns. Direct your partner to the place, starting from the school gates.

51

Costumes

◀**1**  Describing. With a partner, choose one of the pictures opposite, and together prepare a short description of the costumes. Then find a film that you've both liked on television or in the cinema in the past year. Prepare a short description of the costumes in that film.

Change partners. With your new partner, tell each other about the costumes in the two films you chose. Discuss these questions:

1 What do you think the particular problems were in making the costumes for your two films?
2 How important do you think costumes are for you as you watch a film?

Compare your ideas with other students.

Frankenstein

◀**2** Judith Edgeley is a costume specialist in London. Listen to an interview with her. Match the names of the specialists with the pictures that show what each one does.

Costume supervisor Costume designer Assistants

A Making the first drawings

B Discussing the designs with the director and art director

C Choosing the best material

D Making the patterns

E Cutting the material

F Sewing the costumes

Little Women

River Wild

◀3 🗣 Discussion and preparation for listening. With a partner, discuss these questions. Make at least one note about each one.

1 What do you think is most interesting about making costumes for films?
2 What do you think is most difficult?
3 Can you think of any problems?

◀4 📼 The interview continues. As you listen, compare Judith's answers to the three questions with yours. Make notes of a few key words to help you remember her answers. Using your notes, compare your answers with other students.

◀5 📼 Vocabulary work: using context to understand meaning. Here are six idiomatic expressions that Judith uses. Listen to the interview again. Use the context to help you match the phrases in list A with the right meaning in the box.

> **A** 1 absolutely fabulous
>   2 throw a fit
>   3 keep the costs down
>   4 made to last
>   5 quite a lot to think about
>   6 a terrible bore

> **a** durable (something that you can keep for a long time)
> **b** not at all exciting
> **c** be very angy
> **d** rather complicated
> **e** wonderful, beautiful
> **f** make sure it's not too expensive

◀6 🗣 Describing. With a partner, imagine that you are making a film.

- Choose one of these types of film.
  a historical film   a horror film
  a Western   a comedy   a detective story

- Decide on two characters for your film. Give them names. Together, decide on costumes for your two characters.

- Sit with another pair. In turn, describe your characters and their costumes. While you are describing, the others make a very simple drawing of the characters you describe. When you have finished describing, look at their drawing. Did they get it right?

◀7 🗣 Information exchange.

Student A: Look at page 59.
Student B: Look at page 63.

Shooting

◄**1** Before you listen / vocabulary work. You are going to hear an interview with John Roberts, the director of the film *The War of the Buttons*. These are four of the technical terms he uses. With a partner, try to choose the right meanings from the box.

1 to storyboard a scene
2 to shoot a scene
3 to block a scene
4 to rehearse a scene

a to decide on the day of filming how the actors will act and how they will be filmed
b to perform a whole scene, from beginning to end, before filming
c to make a series of drawings which show the way a scene is going to be filmed
d to film a scene

Check the answers with your teacher.

Listen to the interview. In what order are the technical terms used? Number them 1 to 4 as you listen.

◀ **2** 📼 Listening for gist. Listen again and answer these questions.

1 Why were the battle scenes storyboarded?
2 When a scene is blocked, there's no time for one of the other actions above. Which one?
3 Which of these people who work on a film are mentioned by the director?
   a camera operator   **b** costume designer
   c art director   **d** script-writer   **e** actors
4 Two technical terms are used for camera shots: *close up* and *pan*. They are not explained by the director. Which definition is the right one for each?
   a a shot which is very near the person or thing being filmed
   b a shot when the camera is moving

Check your answers with other students, then with the teacher.

◀ **3** 📼 Listening and ordering. Here is part of the storyboard for a scene from *The War of the Buttons*. Listen to the director and the camera operator planning the scene and put the drawings in the right order.

◀ **4** 👄 In a group of four, imagine you are planning to shoot a scene from a film. (You can use the same film as in 12A, exercise 6, or a different one. Your scene has two or three characters.) Plan a scene with some action in it. Prepare a storyboard with about four to six drawings.

Either: perform your scene for another group or the class.

Or: show the class your storyboard and explain how you have planned to shoot your film.

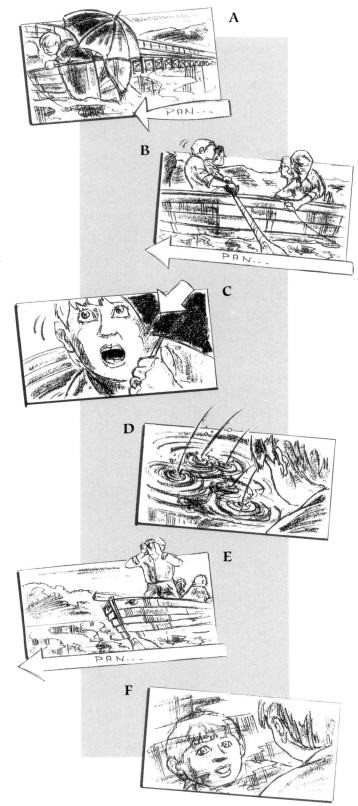

A

B

C

D

E

F

Information exchange activities

◁ **Unit 2B, exercise 6**

1 *Don't* show your page to your partner. Imagine you are a tourist in London and you want information about things to do and see. You start. 'Phone' your partner to enquire about these four attractions. Write down the information.

		Address	Nearest tube station	Opening times	Admission
1	The Science Museum		South Kensington		Adult £3.50 Child £1.75
2	Madame Tussaud's Wax Museum	Marylebone Road, NW1			
3	Changing the Guard		St James' Park		
4	Kew Gardens	Kew, Surrey			

Example:

A: Good morning. Is that the Tourist Information Centre?

B: Yes, it is. Can I help you?

A: Can you give me some information about the Science Museum, please?

B: Certainly. What would you like to know?

A: Where is the Museum please?

B: _____

A: What's the nearest tube station?

B: _____

A: When is it open?

B: _____

A: How much does it cost?

_____

The Tower of London
(Tower Hill, E1)
Historic tower and the Crown Jewels
Nearest tube station: Tower Hill
Open: 9am to 5pm
Admission: adult £8.30, child £5.50

MOMI Museum of the Moving Image
(The South Bank)
A museum of film and television, which offers many things to do
Nearest tube station: Waterloo
Open: 10am-6pm daily
Admission: adult £5, child £4, family (2 adults + 4 children) £16

Museum of London
(London Wall, EC2)
A museum which shows the history of London
Nearest tube station: St Paul's
Open: 10am-6pm Tuesday to Saturday
2pm-6pm Sunday
Admission: free from 4.30pm to 6pm.
All other times, £3

Surrey Docks Farm
(Rotherhithe Street, SE16)
Visit a real farm and see all the animals
Nearest tube station: Rotherhithe
Open: Phone for information: 0171 231 1010
Admission: free from 4.30pm to 6pm.
All other times, £3

2 Now imagine you work at a Tourist Information Centre. Your partner asks you about these four attractions. Give your partner the information.

◀ **Unit 4A, exercise 5**

Don't show your page to your partner. Study the picture of the sports shop. Your partner has a similar picture, but with three things you haven't got. Your picture has three things your partner hasn't got. Ask each other questions, and get the complete list of eight items in the shop.

> *Don't forget: If you don't understand, use a polite expression:*
> I'm sorry?
> I'm sorry, I didn't understand that. Could you repeat it please?
> Could you say that again, please?

◀ **Unit 6B, exercise 6**

Don't show your page to your partner. At eight o'clock last night there was a robbery in a block of flats. The picture shows what some of the people *said* they were doing. But somebody was not telling the truth. Exchange information with your partner and complete the list of what people were doing at eight o'clock last night. Solve the mystery. If there is any contradiction in the information, those people are the robbers. What do you think happened?

What were people doing at eight o'clock last night?	
Flat 1	
Flat 2	
Flat 3	
Flat 4	
Flat 5	
Flat 6	

◀ **Unit 8B, exercise 5**

Don't show your page to your partner.

1 Imagine that you are a travel agent. Your partner wants to book some rooms for different people to visit Edinburgh during the festival. Look at the brochure below and answer your partner's enquiries. Don't forget to apologize if you haven't got what your partner asks for.

> A: Hello. Can I help you?

> B: Yes, I'd like to book some rooms . .

> A: Yes, certainly . ./I'm sorry, we haven't got . .

2 Now you book a holiday in Scotland for these people:

- You and two friends want to book a room in an inexpensive bed and breakfast, for two weeks, from 2nd July to 16th July. You have a dog with you.
- Your aunt and uncle want to book a double room for three days. They don't like single rooms.
- Three of your cousins would like to go to a very inexpensive caravan park near Edinburgh. They've already been to Loch Ness and don't want to go there.

  Your partner is a travel agent who will help you to book the accommodation you want.

> B: Hello. Can I help you?

> A: Yes, please. I'd like to book an inexpensive bed and breakfast. .

Edinburgh accommodation

KEY

🛏	Single rooms only		
🐾	Animals welcome	☆	very inexpensive
⊠	No animals	☆☆	inexpensive
🚗	car parking available	☆☆☆	moderate
🚗̸	no car parking	☆☆☆☆	expensive

EDINBURGH

☆☆☆ **Abbey Inn**
2 David Street

A pleasant old inn with a Victorian bar.

🛏 ⊠ 🚗̸

No rooms available during the festival week

Edinburgh accommodation

☆☆ **MacQueens Hotel**
13 Lothian Street

A comfortable old hotel, with a superb restaurant.

🐾 ⊠

One double room available during the festival week only

☆☆ **Frasers Inn**
25 Princes Street

Very central location.

⊠ 🚗̸ 🛏

Rooms available during the festival

☆ **Waverley House Hotel**
334 Palmers Green

In a quiet suburb of Edinburgh within easy reach of the centre.

🚗 🐾

Rooms available during the festival

◄ **Unit 10A, exercise 6**

Don't show your page to your partner. You have the same map, but with different parts missing.

1 Consult your partner and fill in the missing information on your map of the *Metroland Leisure Complex*.

2 Imagine that you and your partner are spending three hours on Saturday afternoon at the *Metroland Leisure Complex*. You want to do something interesting together. You've got $12 that you can use. Your partner also has some money. Look at the completed map and decide what you'd like to do together.

METROLAND

Leisure Complex

1. OPEN AIR CONCERTS –
ALL THE BEST ROCK BANDS
Saturday 2–4 pm.
Entrance : $10.

2. SKATEBOARDING
Entrance: $6
Rental of protective
equipment: $4.

4 _____
_____
_____
_____

5 _____
_____
_____

3. CYCLING TRAILS
AND HIKING TRAILS
Hiking-free
cycle rental: $3 per hour
Rental of helmets: $1.

◄ **Unit 12A, exercise 7**

Don't show your page to your partner. Look at the three pictures from a film. Your partner has three other pictures from the same film. Together, the six pictures tell the story of the film. Describe your pictures to each other and decide on the right order of the pictures.

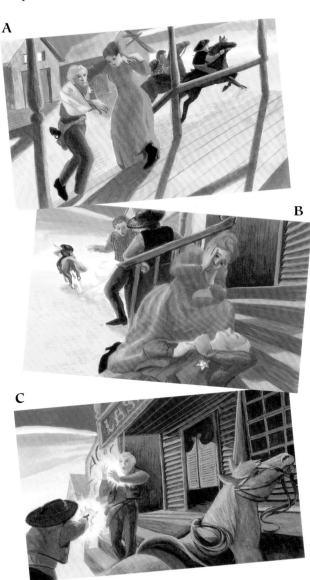

A

B

C

Information exchange activities

◄ **Unit 2B, exercise 6**

Don't show your page to your partner.

1 Imagine you work at a Tourist Information Centre. Your partner begins, and asks you about these four attractions. Give your partner the information.

2 Now imagine you are a tourist in London and you want information about things to do and see. This time you start. 'Phone' your partner to enquire about these four attractions.

Example:

B: Good morning. Is that the Tourist Information Centre?

A: Yes, it is. Can I help you?

B: Can you give me some information about the Tower of London, please?

A: Certainly. What would you like to know?

B: Where is it exactly?

A: _____

B: What's the nearest tube station?

A: _____

B: When is it open?

A: _____

B: How much does it cost?

Madame Tussaud's
(Marylebone Road, NW1)

The famous wax museum, with all the famous people… in wax!
Nearest tube station: Baker Street
Open: 9am-5.30pm every day, July and August
10am-5.30pm Mondays to Fridays,
9,30am-5.30pm Saturday and Sunday September to June
Admission: adult £5.95, child aged 5-15, £3.95

Science Museum
(Exhibition Road, SW7)
A popular museum which lets young people use machines to understand science
Nearest tube station: South Kensington
Open: 10am-6pm, Monday to Saturday
11am-6pm Sunday
Admission: adult £3.50, child aged 5-15 £1.75
family season ticket (2+4) £15

Changing the Guard
(Buckingham Palace, SW1)
The traditional ceremony with guards on horseback
Nearest tube station: St. James' Park
Open: 11.30am daily, April to June
11.30 alternate days (every second day) August-March
Admission: free. Get to the gates of the Palace early to get a good view

Kew Gardens
(Kew, Surrey)
One of the world's greatest collection of plants
Nearest tube station: Kew Gardens
Open: 9.30-dusk (time when it gets dark) daily
Admission: adult £3.30, children (aged 1-12) £1.10

		Address	Nearest tube station	Opening times	Admission
1	The Tower of London	Tower Hill, E1			Adult £8.30 Child £5.50
2	MOMI (The Museum of the Moving Image)		Waterloo		
3	The Museum Of London		St Paul's		
4	The Surrey Docks Farm	Rotherhithe Street, SE16			

◀ **Unit 4A, exercise 5**

Don't show your page to your partner. Study the picture of the sports shop. Your partner has a similar picture, but with three things you haven't got. Your picture has three things your partner hasn't got. Ask each other questions, and get the complete list of eight items in the shop.

> *Don't forget: If you don't understand, use a polite expression:*
> I'm sorry?
> I'm sorry, I didn't understand that. Could you repeat it please?
> Could you say that again, please?

◀ **Unit 6B, exercise 6**

Don't show your page to your partner. At eight o'clock last night there was a robbery in a block of flats. The picture shows what some of the people *said* they were doing. But somebody was not telling the truth. Exchange information with your partner and complete the list of what people were doing at eight o'clock last night. Solve the mystery. If there is any contradiction in the information, those people are the robbers. What do you think happened?

What were people doing at eight o'clock last night?	
Flat 1	
Flat 2	
Flat 3	
Flat 4	
Flat 5	
Flat 6	

◀ **Unit 8B, exercise 5**

Don't show your page to your partner.

A: Hello. Can I help you?

B: Yes, I'd like to book some rooms in Edingurgh, for myself and. .

1 You book a holiday in Edinburgh for these people:

- You and two friends want to book a room at an old inn or hotel in Scotland, for one week, during the Edinburgh festival. You have a cat with you.
- Your parents have asked you to book a double room for the Edinburgh festival. They don't want to be in the suburbs but would like a car parking space.
- Your two cousins would like you to book two single rooms for them during the festival. They want a very central location.

Your partner is a travel agent who will help you to book the accommodation you want.

2 Imagine that you are a travel agent. Your partner wants to book some rooms for a visit to Scotland. Look at the brochure below and answer your partner's enquiries. Don't forget to apologize if you haven't got what your partner asks for.

B: Hello. can I help you?

A: Yes, please. I'd like to book an inexpensive bed and breakfast. .

B: Yes, certainly . . / I'm sorry, we haven't got . .

Scotland accommodation

KEY

 Single rooms only

Animals welcome ☆ very inexpensive

No animals

car parking ☆☆ inexpensive
available

no car parking ☆☆☆ moderate

☆☆☆☆ expensive

SCOTLAND

☆☆☆☆ **Mrs. McThomas**
Loch Lomond

A beautiful guest house on the shores of Loch Lomond.

Rooms available in August only

Scotland accommodation

☆☆ **Clinton House**
Loch Ness

Lovely location near the famous Loch.

Room available from 15th July to 15th September

☆☆ **Duff House**
Loch Lomond

A comfortable hotel with a good restaurant.

Rooms available in June, July and August

☆ **Ness Point Caravan and Camping Park**

5 miles only from Loch Ness: very inexpensive rates.

Rooms available in June, July and August

Unit 10A, exercise 6

Don't show your page to your partner. You have the same map, but with different parts missing.

1 Consult your partner and fill in the missing information on your map of the *Metroland Leisure Complex*.

2 Imagine that you and your partner are spending three hours on Saturday afternoon at the *Metroland Leisure Complex*. You want to do something interesting together. You've got $12 that you can use. Your partner also has some money. Look at the completed map and decide what you'd like to do together.

Unit 12A, exercise 7

Don't show your page to your partner. Look at the three pictures from a film. Your partner has three other pictures from the same film. Together, the six pictures tell the story of the film. Describe your pictures to each other and decide on the right order of the pictures.

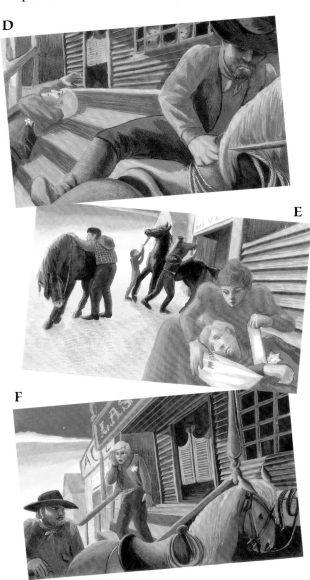

D

E

F

METROLAND

Leisure Complex

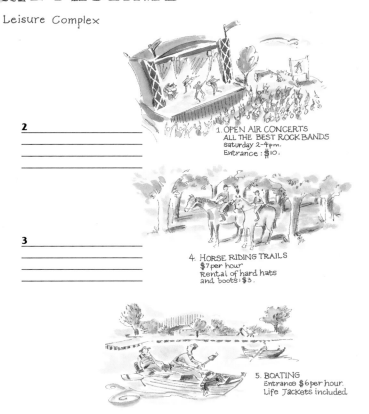

2 _____

3 _____

1. OPEN AIR CONCERTS
ALL THE BEST ROCK BANDS
saturday 2-4pm.
Entrance : $10.

4. HORSE RIDING TRAILS
$7 per hour
Rental of hard hats
and boots: $3.

5. BOATING
Entrance $6 per hour.
Life Jackets included.

Appendix

Unit 2A, exercise 7

Molly Malone

In Dublin's fair City,
Where the girls are so pretty,
I first set my eyes on sweet Molly Malone;
As she wheeled her wheelbarrow
Through streets broad and narrow,
Crying 'Cockles and Mussels, alive, alive-o.'

Alive, alive-o, alive, alive-o,
Crying 'Cockles and Mussels, alive, alive-o.'

She was a fishmonger,
And sure 'twas no wonder,
For so were her father and mother before;
And they both wheeled their barrows,
Through streets broad and narrow,
Crying 'Cockles and Mussels, alive, alive-o.'

Alive, alive-o, alive, alive-o,
Crying 'Cockles and Mussels, alive, alive-o.'

She died of a fever,
And no-one could save her,
And that was the end of sweet Molly Malone;
Now her ghost wheels her barrow,
Through streets broad and narrow,
Crying 'Cockles and Mussels, alive, alive-o.'

Unit 8B, exercise 6

The bonnie, bonnie banks of Loch Lomond

By yon bonnie banks and by yon bonnie
   braes,
Where the sun shines bright on Loch
   Lomond,
Where me and my true love were ever wont
   to go
On the bonnie, bonnie banks of Loch
   Lomond.

Oh, you'll take the high road and I'll take the
   low road,
And I'll be in Scotland before you,
But me and my true love will never meet
   again
On the bonnie, bonnie banks of Loch
   Lomond.

'Twas then that we parted in yon shady glen,
On the steep, steep side of Ben Lomond,
Where in purple hue the Highland hills we
   view
And the moon coming out in the gloaming.

Oh, you'll take the high road and I'll take the
   low road,
And I'll be in Scotland before you,
But me and my true love will never meet
   again
On the bonnie, bonnie banks of Loch
   Lomond.